CHAPTER

1 — John's Vision of Christ — p. 1

- The greeting and first verses identify the sender, the recorder, and the intended recipients of this letter in a grand doxology of praise to the Risen Christ.
- John receives a vision of the glorified Christ on Patmos.
- Christ instructs John to write down the vision in a book.

2-3 — Letters to the Seven Churches — p. 5

- Messages containing praise, correction, and promises to churches in Ephesus, Smyrna
- Pergamum, Thyatira, Sardis, Philadelphia, and Laodicea

4-5 — The Heavenly Throne Room — p. 9

- Glimpse of the throne room and worship in heaven
- The Lamb who was slain is worthy to open the scroll with seven seals.

6 — Opening the Seven Seals — p. 13

- As each seal is opened, a new judgment or calamity is unleashed on the earth.
- Includes conquest, war, famine, death, martyrdom, earthquakes and other calamities.

7 — The 144,000 sealed and the Great Multitude — p. 17

- 144,000 Israelites sealed and protected.
- Vast multitude from every nation worshipped God.

8-11 — The Seven Trumpets — p. 21

- Seven angels blow trumpets, unleashing new waves of judgment.
- Includes hail, fire, locusts, plague, (suggest add and) armies,

12 — The Woman, Child, and Dragon — p. 25

- Woman gives birth to a child who will rule the nations.
- The dragon seeks to devour the child but fails.
- War breaks out in heaven, and the dragon is cast down to earth.

CHAPTER

13 — The Beasts from the Sea and Earth — p. 29
- Beast from the sea with seven heads makes war on the saints.
- Beast from the earth forces people to worship

14 — The Lamb and the 144,000 on Mount Zion — p. 33
- The Lamb and his people stand victoriously on Mount Zion.
- Three angelic messages of judgment and warning

15-16 — The Seven Bowls of Wrath — p. 37
- Seven angels pour out bowls of judgment on the earth.
- Includes painful sores, blood, burning sun, and darkness

17 — The Great Prostitute Babylon — p. 41
- Description of the great prostitute Babylon and her punishment
- Representation of worldly powers opposed to God.

18 — The Fall of Babylon — p. 49
- Lament over the fallen great city of Babylon
- Call to come out of her and not share in her sins.

19 — Rejoicing in Heaven — p. 55
- Celebration in heaven over God judging the great prostitute.
- The marriage supper of the Lamb

20 — Satan Bound and the Thousand Years — p. 59
- Angel binds Satan and locks him in abyss for 1,000 years.
- Saints reign with Christ during this millennium.

21-22 — New Heaven and New Earth — p. 65
- New heaven, new earth, New Jerusalem prepared as a bride.
- The glory of God illuminates the city.
- The river of life and tree of life
- Concluding exhortations

JOHN'S VISION OF CHRIST

The Book of Revelation opens with John explaining that this incredible vision comes directly from Jesus Christ Himself. At the time, Rome had exiled the Apostle John to the island of Patmos for faithfully preaching the gospel. While spiritually immersed and worshiping on the Lord's Day, John hears a loud commanding voice instructing him to carefully write down everything he is about to see and send the record to seven specific churches in Asia Minor.

When John turns to see who is speaking, he has a magnificent vision of the risen Jesus Christ in all His power and glory. John sees Christ with white hair, blazing penetrating eyes, feet glowing like fine bronze, and a voice sounding like the roar of a great waterfall. Jesus appears as the divine, glorified Son of God rather than the Suffering Servant. He declares to John "Do not be afraid!" and identifies Himself as the First and the Last, the Living One who died and returned to life forevermore.

Jesus personally instructs John to record everything in this heavenly vision in a book and send it to seven churches as both encouragement and warning for believers. John then sees seven stars representing the angels, messengers of these seven churches. He also sees seven golden lampstands symbolizing the perfect Holy Spirit dwelling within each church.

In Rev.2:4-5 the Christ warns the church that He would remove their lampstand if they do not repent. It is likely that the seven lampstands represent the churches themselves.

John watches in awe as Jesus holds the seven stars in His right hand and walks among the seven lampstands, signifying His intimate presence and complete authority over the churches. Jesus also tightly grips a sharp double-edged sword representing God's all-powerful word and His face shines brilliantly like the sun in full strength, reflecting His unmatched glory.

Ephesians 6:17, Isaiah 11:4, 2 Thessalonians 2;8 and Hebrews 4:12 all refer to the Word of God as a sharp, powerful sword.

This vivid vision of the risen Christ serves to spiritually prepare readers for the magnificent visions soon to come. It powerfully reveals Jesus as Lord and Head of the Church and identifies Him as the divine source unveiling future events that must soon take place.

NOTABLE VERSES:

- Revelation 1:10-11 - John hears a voice telling him to write what he sees and send it to seven churches.
- Revelation 1:17-18 - "Fear not, I am the First and the Last, and the living One."

KEY STORIES:

- John's Exile and Vision - While exiled on Patmos for preaching Christ, John has an incredible vision of the risen Jesus in glory.

INTERESTING FACTS:

- Revelation is the only book that promises a blessing to those who read and obey it.
- The vision highlights Jesus' divine nature, voice, glory, and authority over the church.

Notes

LETTERS TO THE SEVEN CHURCHES

The resurrected Jesus personally dictates powerful letters to seven specific churches in Asia Minor, containing commendations for their strengths, corrections for their errors, stern warnings of judgment, and incredible promises for those who overcome.

Jesus first commends the Ephesian Church for rejecting false apostles and persevering through hardship. However, Jesus strongly corrects them for losing their first love and passion for Him. He warns this lukewarm church that unless they repent and return to their former devotion, He will remove their lampstand, signifying loss of their light and witness.

The church at Smyrna suffers intense poverty and persecution yet receives no correction from Jesus, only encouragement to remain faithful even unto death.

The church in Pergamum dwells in a city full of pagan idol worship. Yet faithful believers hold fast the name of Jesus. However, Jesus rebukes them for tolerating false teachers and doctrine in their midst. They must repent or else face judgment.

Jesus sternly warns the church at Thyatira against following the teachings and ways of the false prophet, Jezebel, who promotes sexual immorality and idolatrous practices. However, Jesus promises those who remain faithful that they will rule over nations alongside Him in the kingdom.

The church at Sardis has a reputation for being spiritually vibrant and alive. However, Jesus sees through their facade and declares them dead and full of hypocrisy. Only a tiny remnant in Sardis have kept themselves pure. Jesus calls them to wake up immediately and strengthen what little remains before it dies completely.

The church in Philadelphia is weak in strength but strong in faithfulness to God's word, not denying the name of Jesus. As their reward, Jesus promises to protect them from the time of trial and to permanently write the name of His God upon them.

Finally, the lukewarm Laodicean church nauseates Jesus so much that He declares He will spit them out. He instructs them to be zealous and earnestly repent, reopening the door to reestablish fellowship with Him.

These revelatory letters both encourage and sternly warn the churches to remain faithful to Christ and resist conformity amid mounting persecution. Jesus highlights the essential need for sound doctrine, genuine pure love, spiritual wakefulness, and repentance from sin, complacency and unbelief.

NOTABLE VERSES:

- Revelation 2:7 - "To the one who conquers I will grant to eat of the tree of life."
- Revelation 3:20 - "Behold, I stand at the door and knock."

KEY STORIES:

- Letters to Seven Churches - Jesus addresses praises, rebukes, warnings, and promises to seven churches in Asia Minor.

INTERESTING FACTS:

- The letters follow a pattern - commendation, correction, instruction to hear.
- Jesus makes amazing promises to those who conquer trials and temptations through faith.

Notes

CHAPTER 4-5

THE HEAVENLY THRONE ROOM

After writing seven letters to churches, John has a vision of an open door in heaven. He hears the same voice from earlier inviting him to *"come up here"* to be shown future events.

John enters a magnificent throne room and sees Almighty God seated on a glorious jeweled throne encircled by an emerald rainbow. Twenty-four elder saints in white robes with golden crowns surround the throne on lesser thrones. Dramatic lightning, peals of thunder, and rumblings come from the central throne, representing God's awe-inspiring power.

Before the throne is a sea of glass like crystal, along with four living creatures covered with eyes continuously crying *"Holy, holy, holy is the Lord God Almighty!"* Whenever they worship God, the twenty-four elders prostrate themselves in worship and cast their crowns before the throne and declared God alone worthy as the eternal Creator.

John then sees a scroll sealed with seven seals in the right hand of God on the throne. A mighty angel asks loudly *"Who is worthy to open the scroll?"* No one in heaven, earth or the underworld can open it. John weeps no one is worthy.

One elder tells John to weep no more because the Lion of Judah has conquered and is worthy. John then sees a Lamb standing as if slain, yet alive. The Lamb takes the scroll to open the seals as the creatures and elders sing praises, saying He alone is worthy because His blood purchased people for God from every nation.

This vision emphasizes God's supreme glory, holiness, and sovereignty. Yet the Lamb Jesus alone is worthy to complete God's climactic plans by opening the sealed scroll. This sets the stage for the revelations soon to come.

NOTABLE VERSES:

- Revelation 4:11 - Worthy is the Lord God Almighty to receive glory and honor.

- Revelation 5:5, 9 - The sacrificed Lamb is worthy to open the scroll.

KEY STORIES:

- Heavenly Throne Room - John glimpses the awe-inspiring throne room of God surrounded by magnificent creatures giving Him eternal praise and glory.

- The Slain Lamb Takes the Scroll - Though no one else is worthy, the Lamb Jesus takes the scroll signifying his authority over God's plans.

INTERESTING FACTS:

- The throne room imagery draws heavily from Old Testament temple symbols and worship practices.

- Only the slain Lamb is worthy to enact God's final plans, highlighting Christ's supreme authority.

Notes

THE OPENING OF THE SEVEN SEALS

As the Lamb Jesus Christ breaks open the first six of the seven seals securely fastened on the divine scroll, each opened seal sequentially unleashes a new catastrophic judgment upon the earth and its wicked inhabitants. These unfolding judgments represent God beginning to pour out the initial phases of His terrifying wrath upon a sinful, unrepentant world.

The breaking of the first four seals brings forth four ominous horsemen collectively known as the Four Horsemen of the Apocalypse. As the Lamb breaks the first seal, a rider on a white horse appears, carrying a bow and given a victor's crown, riding out as a conqueror bent on conquest and subduing nations. When the Lamb opens the second seal, a rider on a fiery red horse emerges, empowered to take peace from the earth and given a large sword to slaughter people through violence and warfare.

The third opened seal produces a rider on a black horse carrying scales used for measuring grain. The black horse and scales represent widespread economic disaster, high food prices, and scarce famine conditions. As the fourth seal is broken, a rider named Death on a pale sickly green horse appears, followed closely by Hades the grave. These ghostly riders are permitted to kill a massive one-fourth of the earth's population through pestilence, plagues, wild beasts and the sword.

When the Lamp broke open the fifth seal, John saw under the altar the souls of those slaughtered for preaching God's word and the testimony they maintained. These martyrs cry out loudly asking how long before God will judge the earth's inhabitants for murdering them. The martyrs receive white robes and told to rest until their final numbers are complete.

Finally, the breaking of the sixth seal triggers a mighty global earthquake causing every mountain and island to be moved from their places. The sun becomes black as sackcloth, the moon turns blood red, the stars of heaven fall to the earth, the sky itself splits apart like a scroll being rolled up, and every mountain and island is shaken from its place. Seeing these cosmic disturbances, the wicked inhabitants of the earth panic and run in terror, hiding themselves and begging for the rocks and mountains to crush them before the face of God in wrath.

After the opening of the sixth seal, four apocalyptic angels stationed on earth are commanded to hold back and delay the impending release of the four winds of total destruction on land, sea and trees until 144,000 servants of God can be sealed with a protective mark on their foreheads - 12,000 specially chosen and sealed from each of the twelve tribes of Israel.

NOTABLE VERSES:

- Revelation 6:1-2 - The white horse and rider with a bow sent out conquering.

- Revelation 6:12-14 - Global earthquake and the sky recedes like a scroll.

KEY STORIES:

- Four Horsemen of the Apocalypse - The first four seals unleash four horsemen bringing conquest, violence, famine, and death.

- The Great Earthquake - The sixth seal triggers a massive earthquake and signs in the heavens showing God's wrath.

INTERESTING FACTS:

- The colored horses draw from biblical symbols of hardship and war.

- The cosmic disturbances match Old Testament language about God's coming judgment.

Notes

CHAPTER 7

THE 144,000 SEALED & THE GREAT MULTITUDE

Revelation Chapter 7 describes two separate but related majestic visions given to John by God - the protective sealing of 144,000 faithful Jewish servants and a glimpse of a vast, diverse heavenly multitude worshiping Almighty God.

In the first vision, John sees four menacing angels standing at the four corners of the earth. These angels had been prepared to bring about complete destruction to the land, seas, and trees. But another ascending angel cries out with a loud voice, ordering the four angels not to harm the earth until 144,000 servants of God could first be sealed with a protective mark on their foreheads.

12,000 faithful Jewish servants from each of the original twelve tribes of Israel - Judah, Reuben, Gad, Asher, Naphtali, Manasseh, Simeon, Levi, Issachar, Zebulun, Joseph and Benjamin - were to be selected and sealed for protection throughout the upcoming period of global turmoil and devastation about to be released. This vision represents God supernaturally protecting and preserving His own special people on the earth amidst the coming judgments.

After this vision, John then sees an astonishing innumerable multitude of people from every nation, tribe, people, and language standing victoriously before God's throne in heaven. They wear long white victory robes and hold palm branches in their hands, crying out in a loud voice: *"Salvation belongs to our God who sits on the throne, and to the Lamb!"*

All the angels, elders and four living creatures then fall on their faces before God's throne and worship Him together with the great multitude, saying *"Amen! Blessing, glory, wisdom, thanksgiving, honor, and power and might be to our God forever and ever! Amen."*

One of the elders explains to John that these people have come out of the great tribulation on earth; they have washed their robes and made them dazzling white in the blood of the Lamb. Because of this, they are continually before God's throne and worship Him day and night in His temple. The One seated on the throne will shelter them in His presence forever. They will never again hunger, thirst, be scorched by heat or sun, or suffer in any way, for the Lamb will be their shepherd who leads them to springs of living water. And God Himself will tenderly wipe every tear from their eyes.

Together these two interconnected visions portray a God who sovereignly seals and protects His people on earth while also welcoming those redeemed by the Lamb into His glorious presence in heaven to worship Him forever. They offer hope and assurance that though judgments increase, believers will be saved and gather in eternal joyful worship of God and the Lamb.

NOTABLE VERSES:

- Revelation 7:4 - 144,000 servants sealed from every tribe of Israel.
- Revelation 7:9-10 - Vast multitude from all nations worshiping God and the Lamb

KEY STORIES:

- 144,000 Sealed - 144,000 Jewish believers are sealed on their foreheads for protection from coming judgments.
- The Great Multitude - An enormous diverse multitude stands before God's throne having emerged from the great tribulation.

INTERESTING FACTS:

- Some scholars suggest that the 144,000 likely represent the Church completed with converted Jews rather than literally 144,000 ethnic Israelites.
- The great multitude in white robes emphasizes people from all nations united in worshiping God.

Notes

CHAPTER 8-11

THE SEVEN TRUMPETS

With the breaking of the seventh and final seal on the divine scroll, seven angels receive seven trumpets to blow, with each trumpet blast unleashing sequential judgments on the rebellious inhabitants of the earth as warnings of the greater wrath and fury of Almighty God soon to come.

At the blast of the first trumpet, the angels cast down giant hailstones and fire mixed with blood, burning up a third of all the earth's trees and green grass. The second trumpet announces something like an enormous fiery mountain burning with flames being hurled into the sea, turning a third of the sea into blood and killing a third of all sea creatures, and destroying a third of ships.

At the sounding of the third trumpet, a blazing great star called Wormwood falls from heaven, poisoning and bittering a third of all freshwater rivers and springs. When the fourth angel blows his trumpet, a third of the sun and moon and stars lost a third of their light and plunging the day and night into partial darkness.

The sounding of the fifth trumpet opens the Abyss, releasing demonic locusts who are permitted to torture all wicked people without God's seal on their foreheads for five months with agonizing stings but forbidden from killing them. When the sixth trumpet blares, four demons who were bound and imprisoned at the Euphrates River are released to command a monstrous army of two hundred million mounted horsemen with lion's teeth, serpent tails and fiery breastplates to kill a third of all the remaining unrepentant mankind through plague and sword.

In Revelation 10, John sees a mighty angel come down from heaven and stand with one foot on land and one in the sea, holding a small opened scroll. When John ate the scroll as commanded, the scroll tastes as sweet as honey in his mouth but turns sour in his stomach, representing how the Word of God can bring both joy and suffering.

Finally, the seventh trumpet signals that the mystery of God will soon be fulfilled as He reigns forever over the kingdom that shall have no end. When this last trumpet sounds, loud voices in heaven erupt declaring that the kingdom of the world now belongs fully to the Lord God Almighty for all eternity. As the trumpet blasts, lightning flashes, thunder crashes, and a great earthquake convulses the earth as God's heavenly temple opens to reveal the sacred Ark of the Covenant.

Revelation 11 records the ministry of the two prophetic witnesses who testify in Jerusalem for 1,260 days before being slain by the Beast from the Abyss. After 3 1/2 days they are resurrected and ascend into heaven. After they ascend a global earthquake strikes in which 7,000 perish. The second woe is past; the third woe signaling God's final wrath is soon to come.

NOTABLE VERSES:

- 8:10-11 - The star Wormwood poisons the fresh waters.

- 11:15 - Voices declare "The kingdom of the world has become the kingdom of our Lord."

KEY STORIES:

- Seven Trumpets - Angels sound seven trumpets unleashing ecological disasters, demonic torment, armies killing mankind, and finally the reign of Christ.

- Two Witnesses - Two prophets testify for 1,260 days before the beast kills them. They resurrect and ascend to heaven.

INTERESTING FACTS:

- The trumpet judgments parallel the plagues God sent on Egypt before the Exodus.

- One-third destruction shows God's mercy during judgment.

Notes

CHAPTER 12

THE WOMAN, CHILD, AND DRAGON

Chapter 12 provides an important backstory beginning with a vision of a pregnant woman clothed with the sun, with the moon under her feet. A fiery red dragon with seven heads and ten horns appears, ready to devour her child the moment he is born.

The woman gives birth to a male child who is to rule all the nations with an iron scepter. He is caught up to God and to His throne, while the woman flees into the wilderness. There God protects and cares for her during 1,260 days of tribulation when the dragon tries to pursue and overwhelm her with a flood. The 1,260 days likely represent the "time, times and half a time" which is symbolic of 3 1/2 years of persecution.

Next, war breaks out in heaven between the dragon (Satan) and his angels and Michael the archangel with his angels. Satan and his angels do not prevail and there is no longer any place for them in heaven. The dragon is hurled down to earth along with his angels.

Having been thrown down to earth, the dragon is enraged and pursues the woman who gave birth to the male child. But the woman is divinely protected.

Frustrated by his defeat, the dragon makes war against the rest of the woman's offspring on earth who keep God's commandments and remain faithful to Jesus.

Realizing he cannot defeat the male child, the dragon summons a beast from the sea who is given a throne and authority to wage war against God's people and conquer them. The inhabitants of the earth will worship both the dragon and the beast.

This background provides the foundation for the earthly events and judgments soon to unfold. Satan's rebellion results in his banishment from heaven to earth, where he empowers the beasts to deceitfully gain control over the nations and persecute God's faithful people. But God protected them spiritually.

NOTABLE VERSES:

- 12:5 - The woman gives birth to a male child who will rule all nations with an iron scepter
- 12:7-9 - There is war in heaven in which God defeated Satan and cast him to the earth!

KEY STORIES:

- The Woman, Child and Dragon - A pregnant woman gives birth to a son who is caught up to heaven while she is protected from the dragon in the wilderness.
- War in Heaven - Michael and the angels defeated Satan and his angels and cast them out of heaven and down to earth.

INTERESTING FACTS:

- Satan's rebellion results in his banishment from heaven to earth, where he continues to war against God's faithful people.

Notes

CHAPTER 13

29

THE BEAST'S DECEPTIVE REIGN

As the next series of visions begin, John sees a monstrous hybrid beast with seven heads, ten horns, and resembling a leopard, bear, and lion rise arrogantly up out of the chaotic sea. On each of the beast's blasphemous heads is written a name that is contemptuous and irreverent toward God. One of its heads appears to have received a fatal wound, but the deadly wound had been miraculously healed, provoking global wonder, amazement, and worship of the beast.

This beast is given power and extensive authority directly from the dragon (Satan) to act brazenly and blaspheme God, His name, and His tabernacle for forty-two months. The beast savagely makes war against believers in Christ and completely conquers them. All the inhabitants of the earth are compelled to worship the beast and the dragon who empowers it. Every tribe, tongue, ethnicity and nation on earth kneels to worship the beast in awe and adoration.

The beast is allowed to exercise total authority over every people group, language, and nation throughout the world. All earth's inhabitants are forced to worship the murderous beast except those few whose names were written from the foundation of the world in the Lamb's book of eternal life. If any defiant believers are destined for captivity, then into captivity they must go. If any are to die by execution and the sword on account of devotion to Christ, then so they must die. Perseverance, faith, and loyalty to Christ are required by those facing persecution.

Next, John sees a second deceptive beast arising out of the earth itself that has two harmless-looking lamb horns but speaks with the fearsome voice of a fiery dragon. This land beast forces the inhabitants of the globe to worship the first beast from the sea whose fatal wound was healed. The second beast deceives the earth's populace by performing spectacular miracles such as making fire flash down from the sky to the earth as all watch in awe.

The second beast commands the amazed inhabitants of the world to fashion a living, breathing image that honors the first beast who survived a sword strike. The land beast animates the image so it can speak and issue decrees, ordering that any persons refusing to worship the miraculous image must immediately be put to death.

Finally, the deceitful second beast forces all people regardless of status or position to receive an irremovable mark signifying allegiance to the first beast on their right hand or on their forehead. No person could buy, sell, or conduct business of any kind except those having this imposed bestial mark, which is the name of the first beast or his assigned number of 666. Godly wisdom, insightful understanding, and spiritual discernment are needed here, as the number 666 refers to both a specific end times despot along with humanity's imperfection and unholiness in contrast to the divine number 7.

NOTABLE VERSES:

- 13:1 - A beast with ten horns and seven heads rises out of the sea

- 13:16-17 - The Beast forces all people to receive his evil mark on their hands or foreheads.

KEY STORIES:

- The beast from the sea (13:1-8) - This beast blasphemes God, wages war on the saints, and rules over every tribe, tongue and nation.

- The false prophet (13:11-18) - This second beast performs signs and miracles to deceive people into worshiping the first beast and taking his mark.

INTERESTING FACTS:

- 666 is the number of man for humanity, symbolizing human imperfection in contrast to the divine number 7.

- The mark of the beast allows buying, selling, and controls worship. Those who refuse face death.

Notes

THE LAMB AND THE 144,000 ON MOUNT ZION

John looks and sees the Lamb standing victoriously on Mount Zion along with 144,000 redeemed believers who have the Lamb's name and the Father's name supernaturally written on their foreheads. They sing a divinely inspired new song of praise to God before His throne that no one else can learn. An elder declared these 144,000 to be pure, blameless, and redeemed from the earth as first fruits dedicated fully to God and the Lamb. No deceit, fault, or lie could be found in their mouths; their righteousness was perfect.

After this, John sees three sequential angels flying directly overhead in heaven's expanse, each proclaiming eternal gospel truths to the wicked earth-dwellers - to every nation, tribe, language, ethnicity and people.

The first soaring angel commands all on earth to fear God and worship the eternal Creator alone, for the hour of God's judgment has come. A second angel follows, declaring with a mighty voice, *"Fallen, fallen is Babylon the great!"* For Babylon has compelled all nations to drink from her vile immoral passions and has utterly corrupted global society with her brazen idolatry.

A third angel warns in a loud voice that if any person worships the murderous beast and receives his mark, they will certainly drink of the undiluted wine of God's fierce wrath. They will be tormented with fire and burning sulfur in the presence of angels and the Lamb with no rest, for willfully taking the beast's mark displays allegiance to Satan rather than the Creator. This calls for exceptional patience, perseverance, and faith on the part of God's holy people who keep His righteous commandments and remain unwaveringly faithful to Jesus, no matter the cost.

After this, John hears a prophetic voice directly from heaven instructing him to write, *"Blessed are those who from this point die physically in union with the Lord."* The voice says they will permanently rest from all their labors on earth as the record of their deeds endures eternally.

Finally, John beholds a magnificent figure resembling the divine Son of Man seated on a radiant white cloud, wearing a golden royal crown and gripping a sharp sickle in anticipation. A second angel emerges from God's temple in heaven instructing the Son of Man to thrust in His sharp sickle and reap the long-awaited harvest of the earth, for its crops are fully ripe. So, He reaps the earth and gathers in its grapes as a farmer harvests a mature vineyard—this solemn grape harvest represents God's final fierce wrath poured out on sinners. An angel with a sharp sickle harvested the ripened grapes and threw them into the great winepress of God's escalating anger until the flowing lifeblood rises as high as a horse's bridle for 10.2 miles, about the full length of the land of Israel.

NOTABLE STORIES:

- The three angels (14:6-13) - Three angels proclaim the gospel, warn of Babylon's fall, and warn against the mark of the beast.

- Grape harvest of God's wrath (14:14-20) - The Son of Man reaps the harvest of God's judgment, producing a sea of blood.

INTERESTING FACTS:

- 1,600 stadia are about the length of Palestine, implying the extent of God's judgment.

- Mount Zion represents stability, holiness, and was the site of the temple - an appropriate place for God's people.

Notes

CHAPTER 15-16

THE SEVEN BOWLS OF GOD'S WRATH

The apostle John experienced another incredible, awe-inspiring vision in heaven. He sees seven magnificent angels who contained and prepared to pour out the seven final plagues brimming with the full fury of God's impending wrath upon the utterly unrepentant wicked inhabitants of the earth.

John also observes what appeared like a vast sea of glass glowing and shimmering with fire. Standing firmly beside this fiery sea of glass were an untold multitude of joyful and victorious believers who had refused to capitulate or yield to the demands and pressures of the beast. Instead they placed their faith in Christ and His redemptive work. These faithful saints loudly sing two interconnected songs of worship and praise to Almighty God - the liberating song of Moses and the redemptive song of the Lamb. They extol and glorify the Lord God Almighty for His righteous character, righteous acts, righteous ways, righteous judgments, and the manifestation of His divine righteousness through the coming judgments.

After this worship scene, one of the four living creatures approaches the seven angels prepared to dispense God's bowls of wrath and hands each a golden bowl brimming and overflowing with the terrible fury and righteous indignation of God against the utterly wicked.

Then the Sanctuary of God's divine presence and His Majestic glory fills overwhelmingly with smoke arising from the infinite holiness, glory and power of God Himself. No person is able at all to enter the Sanctuary until the seven plagues of God's anger are completed and fully dispensed on the imminent below.

This awe-inspiring vision sets the stage for the seven bowl judgments containing God's final and most intense phase of wrath to be unleashed on the beast's followers. It reveals how heaven is prepared and believers worship the Lord even amid such extreme judgment against defiance of God's reign. It underscores God's uncompromising holiness and righteousness as the basis for the severe judgments about to occur.

NOTABLE STORIES:

- Songs of Moses and the Lamb (15:1-4) - The victorious saints sing praises to God for his salvation and coming judgments.

- Bowls of wrath (16:1-21) - Seven angels pour out bowls bringing agonizing judgments on those who took the mark of the beast.

INTERESTING FACTS:

- The bowls contain the final and most severe of God's judgments.

- Even amid horrific judgments, the unrepentant still refuse to turn to God.

Notes

THE SEVEN BOWLS AND BATTLE OF ARMAGEDDON

The angel poured out the first bowl, causing excruciating sores on those who took the mark of the beast and worshiped his image.

The second angel poured out his bowl into the sea, turning it to blood like a dead corpse. Every living creature in the sea dies.

The third angel poured out his bowl into the rivers and springs, turning them to blood. The angel declares this just vengeance on those who shed the blood of saints.

The fourth angel poured out his bowl on the sun, scorching people with intense fire as punishment for refusing to repent. They curse God's name rather than repent.

Darkness falls over the beast's kingdom as the fifth bowl is poured out on his throne, causing his followers to gnaw their tongues in agony. Their pains and sores cause them to curse God yet still refuse to repent.

The sixth angel poured out his bowl on the Euphrates river, drying it up to prepare the way for the kings of the east. Three unclean spirits in the form of frogs come from the mouths of the dragon, beast, and false prophet, performing signs and gathering the kings of the earth for the battle on the great Day of the Lord!

The term "Day of the Lord" is a widely used prophetic and apocalyptic term suggesting the day of God's wrath on the sin of the earth.

Jesus declares He is coming like a thief when this battle takes place. The spirits gather the kings and their armies at Armageddon.

As the angel poured out the seventh and final bowl loud voices declare, "It is done!" Thunder, lightning, and the worst earthquake ever shake the earth, splitting Babylon into three parts. God remembers to give Babylon the cup of wine of his fierce wrath. Massive hundred-pound hailstones fall from the sky down on people, who continue cursing God because of the terrible plague of hail.

NOTABLE STORIES:

- Bowls of wrath (16:1-21) - The seven bowls bring intensifying judgments on those who took the mark of the beast.

- Battle of Armageddon (16:12-16) - Demonic spirits gather the nations to wage war against God but Jesus warns he is coming like a thief.

INTERESTING FACTS:

- Armageddon means" the mountain of Megiddo." Scripture records significant battles happening there.

- The worst earthquake and hailstorm demonstrate the completeness of God's wrath.

Notes

CHAPTER 17

JUDGMENT ON MYSTERY BABYLON

One of the seven angels who poured out the bowls of God's wrath approaches John. He invites him to witness the impending judgment and downfall of the exceedingly notorious and idolatrous prostitute seated on a scarlet beast arising from chaotic waters. This prostitute symbolizes an apostate world system opposed to God. She has brazenly committed countless immoral acts with the rebellious kings of the earth. She has also intoxicated the inhabitants of the earth with her seductive spiritual idolatry and propagated lies.

John then beholds a marvelous and mysterious sight. He sees an ostentatious prostitute woman seated on a hideous scarlet beast brimming with blasphemous names, having seven heads and ten horns. The extravagantly dressed prostitute wears fine purple and scarlet linens glittering with gold, precious stones, and pearls as a display of wealth and religious significance. In her hand she shamelessly grasps a golden cup overflowing with repulsive abominations and the filth of her vile sexual impurities. Written across her forehead is her title of spiritual degradation: "Babylon the great, mother of all prostitutes and of the earth's abominations."

The immoral prostitute woman is drunk on the spilled blood of God's holy people and on the blood of the martyrs who refused to abandon faith in Jesus, even under threat of death. John views this lurid scene in complete amazement!

The interpreting angel explains that the beast's seven heads represent both seven mountains and seven kings. Five of these kings have already fallen from power, one currently reigns, and the last is still to come and will continue only a short time. The beast empowers the prostitute. The ten horns represent ten additional kings who have not yet received a kingdom but will be granted temporary authority to reign. They will all turn against the prostitute, making her desolate, devouring her wealth and burning her remains with fire. For God has willed it into their hearts to execute His sovereign purpose and destroyed this idolatrous system opposed to His reign.

NOTABLE VERSES:

- 17:1-2 - Judgment on the notorious prostitute Babylon

- 17:12-14 - Ten kings wage war against the Lamb but the Lamb will emerge victorious.

KEY STORIES:

- The prostitute Babylon (17:1-6) - Babylon is dressed in finery, drunk on the blood of saints, provoking wonder.

- The scarlet beast (17:7-14) - The beast and ten kings will hate Babylon, make her desolate, and burn her.

INTERESTING FACTS:

- Babylon represented Rome, center of idolatrous pagan worship.

- God is sovereign, even using evil rulers to fulfill His ultimate purposes.

Notes

CHAPTER 18

THE FALL OF BABYLON

John witnesses another powerful angel radiating brilliant light and having great authority descend from the open heavens. With a mighty and confident voice, the angel loudly proclaims, "*Fallen! Babylon the great has utterly fallen and is permanently destroyed! She has become nothing more than a deserted dwelling-place for repulsive demons and every single foul and unclean spirit.*"

Babylon compelled all the inhabitants and nations of the earth to become intoxicated and insane by drinking the wine of her excessive sensuality, passion for luxury, and unrestrained immoralities. She seduced the kings of the earth into committing illicit sexual acts of every kind with her. The global merchants and traders of the earth have also amassed limitless wealth by catering to her constant cravings for extravagance, excess, and luxury.

Next, John hears an additional prophetic voice directly from heaven, calling for God's holy people remaining in Babylon to immediately come out and be separate from her. This urgent warning is so believers do not share in any of Babylon's escalating sins, participate in any of her immoral pleasures, or receive any of her impending plagues and judgments about to crash down on her from God in fury.

For Babylon's voluminous sins and crimes against morality have amassed clear to heaven itself. God has not forgotten any of her unrestrained wicked deeds but will repay her back double in severity for all she has arrogantly done. Judgment day has arrived.

The kings of the earth who committed unrestrained sexual immorality with her and participated in her excessive global luxury will weep in despair and wail in agony when they gaze from a safe distance at the smoke rising from her fierce and raging fire of destruction. They will cry out, "*Alas, alas for your terrible fate, O great and mighty city, O Babylon, city of power! For in a single decisive hour your long-awaited judgment has at last arrived!*"

The global merchants who expanded their wealth through catering obsessively to her insatiable consumer demands will also bitterly weep in despair and mourn over her complete annihilation. For no one any longer buys their vast arrays of merchandise: gold, silver, precious stones, pearls, fine fabrics of linen, silk, and purple, all kinds of expensive citrus woods, bronze, iron, marble, cinnamon, unique spices, costly perfumed incense, myrrh, frankincense, extravagant wine, olive oil, the finest flour, livestock including cattle, sheep, horses, and even human slaves.

THE FALL OF BABYLON *(CONT...)*

In barely an hour, all of Babylon's excessive riches have been laid completely waste and will never be found again.

Every ship's captain, sailor, and all who profit from working the sea will stand far off, crying out in horror and mourning when they witness thick black smoke ominously rising high from her raging fire of destruction. They will pathetically pour dust on their heads as was the ancient custom and weep bitterly over this great luxurious city, crying, "Was there ever such a city as this!" In barely an hour, it has been left completely desolate and destroyed."

Finally, John watches a mighty angel dramatically seize an enormous millstone the size of a massive boulder and violently hurl it into the sea. This symbolic action signifies that Babylon the prostitute will never ever be found again. All the sounds of craftsmen busily plying their trades, the noise of grinding flour at the mill, the bright lights of wedding parties, and the cacophony of musicians playing divers instruments will never ever be heard at all in her again. For in one brief hour, she has been made totally and permanently desolate

NOTABLE VERSES:

- 18:4 - God's people called to come out of Babylon and not share in her punishment
- 18:10 - In one hour your judgment has come!

KEY STORIES:

- Babylon's judgment (18:1-24) - Babylon is laid waste and destroyed, provoking mourning from the kings and merchants who profited from her.

INTERESTING FACTS:

- Babylon represents worldly luxury, self-indulgence and sinful pleasures.
- God repays her double for her sins and wipes her off the earth.

Notes

Notes

CHAPTER 19

55

REJOICING OVER BABYLON'S FALL

After Babylon's destruction, a great multitude in heaven exclaims *"Hallelujah! Salvation and glory and power belong to our God, for his judgments are true and just."* The twenty-four elders and four living creatures worship God, agreeing that Babylon has been judged. Again they shout *"Hallelujah! The Lord our God the Almighty reigns! Let us rejoice and exult and give him glory!"*

Then John hears the roar of a great multitude, like rushing waters and loud peals of thunder, crying *"Hallelujah! For the Lord, our God the Almighty reigns. Let us rejoice and exult and give him glory."*

The twenty-four elders and four living creatures worship God, crying *"Amen, Hallelujah!"* A voice instructs all God's servants to praise him, small and great.

John then hears the roar of a great multitude, like rushing waters and peals of mighty thunder, shouting: *"Hallelujah! For the Lord, our God the Almighty reigns. Let us rejoice and exult and give him glory, for the marriage of the Lamb has come, and his Bride has made herself ready."* The marriage of the Lamb has come, and his bride clothed herself in fine linen, bright and pure representing the righteous deeds of the saints.

John is instructed, *"Blessed are those who are invited to the marriage supper of the Lamb."* John attempted to worship the angel but was told to only worship God, for the testimony of Jesus is the spirit of prophecy.

Then heaven opens and Christ rides out on a white horse followed by the armies of heaven to strike down the nations and rule them with an iron scepter. An angel summons birds to feast on the flesh of those slain. The beast and false prophet are captured and thrown into the lake of fire.

NOTABLE VERSES:

- 19:6-9 - Praise God for the wedding of the Lamb has come!
- 19:11-16 - Christ rides out followed by the armies of heaven.

KEY STORIES:

- Songs of praise (19:1-8) - Multitudes in heaven rejoice and praise God for judging Babylon and for the wedding feast.
- The marriage supper (19:9-10) - The bride wears righteous deeds and blessed are those invited to the feast.

INTERESTING FACTS:

- The marriage feast illustrates Christ's intimate relationship with his people.
- The bride is given fine, bright linen representing righteous acts.

Notes

CHAPTER 20

THE THOUSAND YEAR REIGN AND THE RAPTURE DEBATE

John beholds a mighty angel descending from heaven possessing the key and chain to lock the bottomless Abyss. The angel forcefully seizes Satan, that ancient serpent of old also called the devil, and powerfully binds him in chains. The angel throws Satan into the locked Abyss to keep him from deceiving all the nations of the earth until the prophetic thousand years are completed and finished.

After this, John sees glorious thrones on which those given authority to judge are seated upon. He also sees the souls of those saints who had been martyred and beheaded because of their faithful testimony about living for Jesus and proclaiming the word of God. These martyrs had refused to worship or bow down to the murderous beast or his image. Neither had they received his mark upon their hand or forehead. The martyrs come back to life again and reign victoriously with Christ for a thousand years as priests of God. This resurrection is designated as the first resurrection into new eternal life. The second death which is eternal separation from God holds no power over these resurrected saints whatsoever. Instead they will rule and reign alongside Jesus Christ for the entire thousand years.

When the prophetic thousand years have ended, Satan will be briefly released once more from his prison in the Abyss. He will go forth immediately to deceive and mislead the nations and peoples living in the four corners of the earth, gathering them together for one final epic battle. This massive army will surround and march across the broad plains to attack the beloved city of God. But fire directly from heaven will flash down and completely devour them. And the devil who deceived them will be thrown permanently into the fiery and burning lake of sulfur, to be tormented both day and night continuously and forever without end.

Next John beholds a magnificent great white throne looming in heaven with the infinitely holy One seated upon it in glory. The newly restored earth and expansive heavens immediately flee away from His holy unveiled presence, so there is no place found for them anymore. All the dead stand fully exposed before the glorious throne, regardless of status or rank while they lived. The intently scrutinizing books containing full records of everyone's deeds will be carefully opened for review. Finally, physical Death itself and Hades, the realm of the dead, will be hurled into the fiery lake of burning sulfur. This represents the second death which is eternal separation from God. And all whose names were not found written in the Lamb's book of eternal life are sentenced and thrown into the lake of unquenchable fire along with Death and Hades.

THE THOUSAND YEAR REIGN AND THE RAPTURE DEBATE *(CONT...)*

There is considerable disagreement among believers about precisely when the future rapture or catching away of the Church into heaven occurs in relation to end times events. Some contended it happens before the tribulation, others say it will occur only after the millennium. There are various conflicting interpretations about its exact timing

NOTABLE VERSES:

- 20:1-3 - An angel binds Satan and locks him in the Abyss for 1,000 years
- 20:11-15 - The great white throne judgment of all people according to deeds

KEY STORIES:

- Satan bound (20:1-3) - An angel binds Satan in the Abyss so he cannot deceive the nations for 1,000 years.
- The millennium (20:4-6) - Those martyred for Christ are resurrected to reign with Him 1,000 years on the earth

INTERESTING FACTS:

- This is the only place in Scripture mentioning a thousand year reign of Christ on earth.
- There are various views about when the rapture of believers happens in relation to end times events.

Notes

Notes

CHAPTER 21-22

A NEW CREATION AND THE NEW JERUSALEM

John sees a new heaven, new earth, and New Jerusalem prepared as a bride adorned for her husband. A loud voice proclaims God's dwelling is now among people, and He will dwell with them as their God. He will wipe away every tear. He will make all things new.

The One on the throne declares, "*Write this down, for these words are trustworthy and true: It is done! I am the Alpha and the Omega, the Beginning and the End.*" Those who overcome will inherit these things, while the unrepentant will face the second death in the lake of fire.

An angel shows John the holy city Jerusalem coming down out of heaven from God, shining with His glory. It gleams like a precious jewel with walls, twelve gates of single pearls, and streets of transparent gold. The glory and honor of the nations will be brought into it.

The city needs no temple or sun because God Almighty and the Lamb illuminate it. The kings of the earth will bring their splendor into it and its gates will never shut.

The angel shows John the river of the water of life flowing from God's throne, and the tree of life bearing fruit for the healing of the nations. The throne of God and the Lamb will be in the city. His servants will worship Him and reign forever.

Jesus testifies saying, "*Behold, I am coming soon*" to reward the righteous and judge evildoers. He proclaims, "*I am the Alpha and the Omega, the first and the last, the beginning and the end.*" He invites the thirsty to freely drink the water of life.

NOTABLE VERSES:

- 21:1-4 - A new heaven and earth, God dwells with man, no more death or mourning

- 22:1-2 - The river and tree of life in the New Jerusalem

KEY STORIES:

- The New Jerusalem (21:9-27) is an incredible holy city made of pearls, gold, and precious stones from heaven.

- The river and tree of life (22:1-5) - Flowing from God's throne, the tree and river provide healing for the nations.

INTERESTING FACTS:

- The New Jerusalem is described as a perfect cube about 1,400 miles wide, long, and tall.

- Eternity with God is finally realized as He dwells face-to-face with redeemed humanity.

Notes

Made in the USA
Monee, IL
05 August 2024

63277257R00044